Weird, Wacky & Wonderful

Amazing World Records

Marg McAlister

Contents

ETA Cuisenaire

Introduction

You can set **world records** in lots of things.

You don't have to be very brave or very sporty. You don't have to be the oldest person in the world. You don't have to be the strongest person in the world. You don't have to be very talented… or even very clever!

You might think some world records are actually a bit stupid. How many worms could you eat in thirty seconds? How many worms would you want to eat in thirty seconds?! Mark Hogg of Kentucky set a world record for eating worms. He ate sixty-two worms in thirty seconds— on prime-time TV!

There are 500 worms on this plate. How many could you eat in thirty seconds?!

John Evans 27 Times

To set a world record, you don't have to eat worms. There are lots of things you can do.

Think in terms of these words: *longest*, *shortest*, *biggest*, *smallest*, *most*. Maybe you could write the longest letter in the world. Maybe you could have the world's biggest ant farm. Maybe you could collect the most grains of sand. (Imagine counting those!)

Just for fun, we'll look at all sorts of amazing records. Some are dangerous. Some are funny or weird. Some records were set in seconds…and some took years!

John Evans holds the world record for balancing heavy objects on his head! Find out more on page 18.

The S-l-o-w-e-s-t and the Fastest Records

Fastest

Brrrrr ... what a cool record!

Frozen in Time

When everything gets too fast, it's time to chill out. And what better way to chill out than sitting inside a block of ice for a few days? You don't have to race against anyone or anything else—except time!

That's exactly what **illusionist** David Blaine did. He sat inside a six **ton** block of ice for sixty-two chilly hours—right in the middle of Times Square, New York.

A medical team watched David closely as he shivered his way to a record. When the **stunt** finished, the team wrapped David in blankets and took him to a hospital in an ambulance to recover.

4

Man Talks Head Off!

How fast do you talk? Most people talk at sixty words a minute. That's about one word per second. Steve Woodmore of Kent, England, set a world record for fast talking. He spoke 637 words in one minute! That's over ten times faster than most people talk.

Steve made a radio advertisement for a supermarket chain. For the advertisement, he spoke at 380 words a minute. (If he'd spoken any faster, no one would have understood him!)

Knot That Fast!

Maybe you think that talking fast is easy. Maybe you think that tying knots is easy, too. Look at these six knots; they look simple, don't they?

1. The square knot
2. The sheet bend
3. The sheepshank
4. The round turn and two-and-a-half hitches
5. The clove hitch
6. The bowline

How long would it take you to tie one of these knots? About a minute? Clinton Bailey from Oregon tied all six knots in just 8.1 seconds! He tied each knot on separate ropes. No one has beaten his record since 1977. Could you beat it?

1 Square knot

2 Sheet bend

3 Sheepshank

4 Round turn and two-and-a-half hitches

6 Bowline

5 Clove hitch

The Most Dangerous Records

Highly Strung Heroes

Lots of people can ride a motorcycle. Quite a few people can swing on a trapeze. A number of people can do tricks on a high wire.

But how many people can do all of these things at once—650 feet above the ground? Not many!

At Tournemire Cirque in France, two **tightrope** artists, Pascal Barrier and Jacques Steinmesse, performed tricks on a high wire while 3,000 nervous people watched below. The high wire was stretched out between two cliffs. One artist rode the motorbike across the wire; the other did tricks on the trapeze hanging below the motorbike.

Woman Blows Herself Up!

Would you hop into a box and blow yourself up? No? Well, Allison Bly would. Allison calls herself the "Dynamite Lady." She has blown herself up more than 1,500 times! (Amazingly, Allison is still in one piece and has all her arms and legs.)

Allison uses a box she calls the "Coffin of Death." The explosives she uses are equal to two sticks of **dynamite**.

Coffin of Death

I can think of better ways to have fun!

Snakes Alive!

Do you get bored when you are home alone? You can make it more interesting... by inviting some **rattlesnakes** to join you!

Boonrang Buachan spent one whole week with one hundred rattlesnakes in a glass room. No doubt, this record will be held by Boonrang for a long, long time.

I guess 's what you'd ll a real snake charmer!

That's Really Weird!

Do you still want to set a world record? But you don't want to blow yourself up or spend a week with rattlesnakes. Well, there are other ways of setting world records. Be careful—some of them are really weird!

The World's Strongest Man

If you want to be the world's strongest man, you'd better start building up those muscles. The current world-record holder, Magnus Magnusson, from Iceland, is so strong that he can pull a truck using a rope attached to his waist!

Magnus set the world record on July 23, 2000, at the World's Strongest Man contest in St Louis, Missouri. If you want to find out more, see the **Story Surfers CD-ROM** for the Web address.

Juggling Act

Long ago, farmers used **scythes** to cut down crops in the fields. Not Henri St. Étienne! Known as the World's Most Fantastic Rope-Dancer, Henri juggled three scythes for twenty-four hours. Perhaps not surprisingly, he has held this record since 1965.

Well, it's more fun than arm wrestling!

Woman Pops Eyeballs!

When you see something that gives you a shock, do your eyes pop? Most of us open our eyes wide. Sometimes our eyes bulge out a bit. They probably don't bulge as much as Kim Goodman's eyes.

Kim, from Illinois, can make her eyes really **Pop!** They pop out about half an inch! Her eyes look like golf balls that are about to fall out of her head! You can see Kim in action on the Internet. Check the **Story Surfers CD-ROM** for the address.

9

Stunts on Wheels

Man Defies Gravity!

How long can you do a **wheelie** on your bike? Can you last maybe three or four minutes? Well, Kurt Osburn of California can beat that. Kurt set the world record in 1998 by doing a wheelie on his bike—for eleven hours!

I wonder how many back tires he used up?

Then Kurt wanted more of a challenge. He wanted to be the first person to wheelie all the way across the United States of America!! In 1999, Kurt rode from Hollywood, California, to Orlando, Florida. That's 2,832 miles. Kurt did his wheelies for 50 miles at a time. Phew! It's hard enough to ride 50 miles on two wheels, without having to do a wheelie as well!

Man Rides Backwards!

Christian Adam, of Germany, likes to play the violin. He likes riding his bike, too. So Christian got dressed up in a formal suit. He put the music sheets on the back of his bike. Then he got on his bike, with his violin, and started pedaling… backwards!

Christian Adam and Kurt Osburn should share a bike. Kurt could do wheelies and watch Christian play violin!

Christian Adam cycled backwards for 70 miles, playing his violin all the way.

Skater Speeds to Record!

Falling off a skateboard hurts. The faster you're going, the more it hurts. So imagine travelling at over 60 miles per hour! Gary Hardwick from California set a world record in 1998 with this speed. Gary was lying down on his skateboard so that he would not have as much wind resistance!

Gary Hardwick sliding through a **hairpin switchback** on his way to a world record

11

Fun and Games

Mosaic Madness

What can you do with a whole lot of jellybeans?
1 You can eat them. (But not too many, or you'll get sick.)
2 You can put them in a jar and hold a "Guess How Many Jellybeans" competition.
3 You can make a giant mosaic picture with them and win a world record!

On 19 April, 2000, Stephanie Logan of California made a world-record-sized mosaic using jellybeans. Stephanie used 210,000 jellybeans! (Imagine counting those...) Her jelly-bean picture of two happy rabbits contained 798 pounds of candy.

Does anyone want to buy 210,000 used jellybeans? Going cheap!

Man Hops in Sleep!

How good are you at playing **hopscotch**? Are you good enough to play non-stop for twenty-four hours? Ashrita Furman can.

In 1998, he played 434 games of hopscotch in Cancun, Mexico, without stopping. Wow! A world record!

Man Chews Lots and Lots of Gum!

Gary Duschl from Ontario, Canada, holds the record for the longest gum-wrapper chain. He started it thirty-five years ago. And just to make it harder, he uses only one brand of chewing gum wrappers. Gary gets people to send him their gum wrappers. He even asks them to sign the wrappers.

Early in 2001, Gary's gum-wrapper chain was 11,990 yards long. It weighed about 463 pounds and took up lots of space! If Gary's chain were stretched out beside a road, a car would have to drive at about 60 miles per hour for five minutes to pass it. Check Gary's website to find out how long his gum-wrapper chain is now. See the **Story Surfers CD-ROM** for the address.

I hope he likes chewing gum!

Tall Tiny Tower

One of the world's tallest Lego buildings was made in Cascais, Portugal, in 1992. It took 2,000 children more than sixteen-and-a-half hours to build it. The building was over 64 feet high. That's as tall as ten people standing on each other's shoulders! Altogether, 250,000 blocks were used to make the building.

Giant Millipede Threat!

The longest Lego structure ever made is a **millipede**. Millipedes are small insects, but this millipede was 631 yards long! (That's as long as 320 people lying feet to head, all in a row.) It was made in the Czech Republic in 1998 by 20,000 people. So start practicing with your Lego blocks—it might be your turn to break the record!

Dance Fever Breaks Out!

Do you like dancing? There are lots of chances to break records here! You can tap dance…or do the chicken dance…or do some **line dancing**! Just get together with a few thousand other dancers. A world record could be yours!

In Tamworth, Australia, 6,275 people joined together in a country line dance. They danced to "Bootscootin' Boogie." That was in January 2000.

In 1996, 72,000 people did the chicken dance at the Canfield Fair in Ohio. So get your dancing shoes on—and hotfoot your way into the record books!

Tappity-tappity-tap, kick!

Crazy Collections!

It's fun collecting things. It's also one of the easiest ways to set a world record. You can ask your friends to help add to your **collection**. Most collectors run out of room to keep their collection. I hope you've got a big, big garage ...

The Human Pin Cushion!

Badges are fun and easy to collect. But if you want to hold the world record in badge collecting, don't waste too much time.

George Brinacombe of Somerset, England, started his collection when he was a small boy—fifty-seven years ago. Now he has more than 5,000 badges!

George has so many badges that it can be hard to see him under them all! That's why he wears a bright red wig.

Have you got a badge with me on it?

Magnets Attract Girl!

Fridge magnets are easy to collect! They're everywhere. You could easily get the best collection in your street. Or the best collection in your class. Or even the best collection in your suburb! But first, you would have to beat the world-record holder.

The world-record holder is Louise Greenfarb of Washington. Louise has over 29,000 fridge magnets.

Louise would need about 100 fridges to put her magnets on. And a lot of kitchens to hold the fridges. And a lot of houses to hold the kitchens ...

Guaranteed Garage-Fillers!

Here are some other things that world-record holders collect:

- dolls
- clothing tags
- golf balls
- mugs
- garden gnomes
- bus tickets
- airplane sickbags.

What can *you* collect?

You collect sickbags? Yuk! I hope they're empty!

Fame at Last!

Lots of people who hold world records become famous. Some world-record holders have their own websites, so that people can find out about their latest **exploits**.

Man Balances Car on Head!

John Evans can hold amazingly heavy things on his head—he can even hold a car! He's also held on his head 400 cans of drink, and a person sitting on a chair! John holds the record for balancing the most people on his head in one hour. How many? Ninety-two people! (One at a time, of course!) He set this record in Lowestoft, England, in 2000.

John has appeared on television in thirty-eight countries. You can find his Web address on the **Story Surfers CD-ROM**.

That's using your head!

Man Puts Head in Clouds!

Doug the Great holds the record for walking on the tallest **stilts**. His stilts were 51 feet high!

Doug works as an entertainer. He walks on stilts. He puts on a magic show and shows people how to juggle.

If you set a world record, like Doug, it could lead to a new career! You can find out more about Doug on the Internet. Check the **Story Surfers CD-ROM** for his Web address!

Man Breaks Records for Breaking Records!

Ralf Laue of Leipzig, Germany, likes breaking records. You can see that if you visit the **Rekord-Klub Saxonia** website. Ralf has a long list of records. He has held world records for:

1 Holding the largest fan of cards
   Ralf held a fan of 326 cards.

2 Creating the largest magic square
   Ralf's magic square was 2121 x 2121 numbers! It added up to the same number vertically, horizontally, and diagonally.

3 Domino stacking
   Ralf stacked an incredible 555 dominoes. (You can find out more about domino stacking on page 20.)

4 Calendar memorising
   Ralf worked out which days of the week were on which dates, for a whole year… in just 222 seconds!

5 Letter opening
   Ralf opened 1,000 letters in twenty-nine minutes and three seconds.

6 Pancake tossing
   Ralf tossed 416 pancakes in three minutes.

> I wonder how many pancakes stuck to the ceiling?

Record Club Membership!

Most clubs have conditions about joining. The Rekord-Klub Saxonia has membership conditions, too.

Before you can join the club, you need to be a world-record breaker. Every member of the club has broken a world record.

You can visit Rekord-Klub Saxonia on the Internet. Check the **Story Surfers CD-ROM** for the address. If you look hard, you might find a record you can break!

Try Beating These Records!

Most world records are based on doing simple things quickly—or for a long time! Here are some activities that anyone can try.

Domino Stacking

Domino stacking is quite hard. You have to start off with just one domino. It has to stand upright on the thin edge. Then you stack the other dominoes on top, lying flat. You are not allowed to use any glue!

In 1999, Ralf Laue of Germany set a new world record. He built a stack of 555 dominoes, all balanced on the first one. It stayed up for an hour. Beat that!

Ball Juggling

There are lots of world records for this! Even if you can't set a world record, you might set a school record. Try these:

1 Controlling a Soccer Ball

How long can you keep a soccer ball in the air? There are three conditions.

- You must be moving.
- You can't use your hands.
- You must be standing upright.

The world record is twenty-four hours and thirty minutes!

2 Juggling a Soccer Ball

This sounds easy, doesn't it? But there's a catch. You have to **juggle** sitting down—without using your hands! You can only use your shoulders, head, thighs, knees, or arms. The world record is one hour and nine minutes.

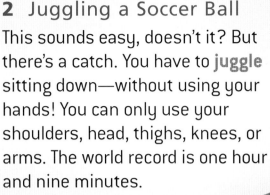

3 Heading a Soccer Ball: Doubles Passing

This is two people working together, using only their heads to pass a soccer ball to each other. The world record is 3,455 times. The record has stood since 1972.

4 Juggling a Tennis Ball with Your Feet

The record is one hour, twenty-five minutes, and eleven seconds. You don't need any fancy equipment, so start practicing now!

Why not have a school "Records Day"? You can try these skills with balls of different sizes, such as tennis balls and ping-pong balls. Decide on the categories. Plan it early. And see if you can win!

So You Want to Set a World Record?

You can be in the next edition of the *Guinness Book of Records*! All you have to do is work with your friends to break a record. Look for a safe record to break. The *Guinness Book of Records* (and the publisher of this book) does **not** want people to risk their lives!

1 Provide proof of your attempt, such as a videotape of the record-breaking attempt. (You might need to show a clock in the background.)

2 You must have at least two independent witnesses. These people must not be related to you. They should be people who are respected in your community, such as doctors, police officers, or leaders of sporting organizations.

3 You might need an expert to witness your attempt.

4 Apply early to the *Guinness Book of Records*. Tell them what you are going to do. Check their guidelines. Check the **Story Surfers CD-ROM** for the *Guinness Book of Records* Web address.

5 Before you start, check that the record has not just been broken!

Good luck with your record attempt! Don't forget to have fun!

Glossary

collection a group of items, such as stamps, that are kept as a hobby

dynamite an explosive used for blowing up rocks and buildings

exploit something a person has done or achieved

Guinness Book of Records a book that lists world records

hairpin switchback a skateboard move through a tight corner or bend

hopscotch a game in which players hop in a pattern of squares

illusionist a person who uses magic tricks to do "impossible" feats

juggle to keep an object moving in the air

line dance a dance where everyone stands in a line

millipede an insect with lots of pairs of legs

rattlesnake a poisonous snake with a rattle in its tail

Rekord-Klub Saxonia a club for people who hold world records

scythe a long curved blade with a wooden handle; used for harvesting crops

stilts long wooden or metal poles that attach to your legs

stunt a daring and dangerous activity

tightrope a wire stretched high above the ground; used for performing tricks

wheelie to ride with the front wheel of your bike in the air

world record the best in the world; often listed as the heaviest, the fastest, and so on

Index